EASY DOES IT

AKRON SERIES IN POETRY

EASY DOES IT

JENNIFER MOORE

The University of Akron Press
Akron, Ohio

ISBN: 978-1-62922-207-3 (paper)
ISBN: 978-1-62922-212-7 (ePDF)
ISBN: 978-1-62922-213-4 (ePub)

A catalog record for this title is available from the Library of Congress.

∞ The paper used in this publication meets the minimum requirements of ANSI/NISO
z39.48–1992 (Permanence of Paper).

Cover image: *The Long Study of the Sea* by Matthias Jung (www.zabadu.de)
Cover design by Amy Freels.

Easy Does It was designed and typeset in Minion with Futura titles by Amy Freels and
printed on sixty-pound natural and bound by Bookmasters of Ashland, Ohio.

Produced in conjunction with the University
of Akron Affordable Learning Initiative.
More information is available at
www.uakron.edu/affordablelearning/.

CONTENTS

For Mom

Let us consider through what clouds and how gropingly we are led to the knowledge of most of the things that are right in our hands.

—Montaigne

GRAND OPENING

And now the guests are arriving,
two by two by two. Somebody mists the lilies.
Every marble column's veined in grey.

I was cordially invited to attend this event;
I play it very cool. I stroke my invisible beard
and strike up a conversation with a sculpture.

I like drinks. I like corners.
Of course I care about art!
In my heart, I'm pawing at the air.

I try to describe what I'm seeing.
I try to think about colors,
about what catches my eye

and why. To be honest,
it's the hundreds of napkins
folded into swans, swimming on each table.

The newest museum piece is flanked
by impressionist paintings; the crowd jostles in.
They snap a shot, grab a drink, and walk away.

An ice sculpture drips into a sagging mess.
My heels punch through the manicured grass.
At least I can make limping look natural, simple.

I peer back into the museum's halls,
no clue where the latest marvel is.
Every impression looks the same to me:

their blues and greens are soothing,
but I want to be the vein in the marble,
the only thing interrupting its purity.

Day turns the corner into evening.
Everybody had a great time looking good.
The paintings hang, unwatched, in the dark.

OF WHAT'S DIFFICULT

Things are tough all over.
I've just been notified that my cloud
is completely full.
Even the dog just wants to be left alone.

We try to muddle through,
somehow. I rehang last year's calendar
just to spite this year.

Someone tags me in a post:
If you haven't yet voted
for the best album of 1993, now's the time!
The dog walks out of the room.

On TV, someone places a crown of flowers
on the head of a serial killer.

In the meantime, what am I supposed to do
with these balloons?
How much cocoa do I add
to the boiling water?
Pleasure is anyone's guess.

All I want is for someone to drop
a cherry into my cocktail, mid-sip.
It's the little things I miss
about all of my future desires.

Even the sloth, smiling serenely,
must be escorted across the road
or risk being flattened by a tourist.

Like everything else, it takes longer
to de-ice the wings
than it does to fly home.

I HAVE NO WAY WITH WORDS

I have no way with words. A chill has stopped my mouth.
Press the button for the elevator: it never arrives.

I refuse sunflowers. I chase my own tail.
In the mirror: no eyes no lashes no lips.

For the Neverland boy who lost his shadow, soap will do the trick.
Sit in the corner, kid; rub the cake on the sole of your foot.

Wendy knows better. Only a needle and thread
can reattach silhouette to self, self to mind—

but without a mechanism to hook
syllable to sound, then thing to thought,

my language lies loose, and every nameless animal
worries itself away. At a loss, these walls don't mourn,

but this is my house. Muse of Silence,
here's your muzzle back. I'll go as a ghost goes:

tying a white feather to the hornet,
I'll follow its flight back into the nest. You'll know

my voice when you see it: a seedling hatching honey.
An egg whose blue mouth has flown open.

BY DEFINITION

I like my water not too wet, my sugar not too sweet.
What's *possible* is overrated. Give me the cool fire instead.

Give me the cool fire, the impossible scheme,
the authority to speak as timidly as I want to.
There's plenty of room under this closed umbrella,

but it's not my job to lead a horse to water.
Wait, is it my job to lead a horse to water?
Rarely do I put two and two together.

When I *do* put two and two together, though,
the four winds blow cold, and all at once.
I'm afraid of the life I've chosen. Self, of course,

is the consequence of self: impossible to be no worse for wear,
less so to be a fire, defined by what shivers around it.

FOOL ME TWICE

Beggars can't be choosers, said the chooser to the beggar.
Challenge accepted. I call the coin in the air.

The air itself isn't so clear. Fog is a cloud
that touches the ground; fog is a cloud that is near.

Some things you can't control. This nickel, for instance,
bearing two tails. I accept the only offer given.

Yes, I prefer the rock to the hard place.
Yes, the hard place resembles the rock.
Actually, this *is* my first rodeo.

I raise my hand, then have nothing to say.
When called on to answer, the tongue stops short.
The mouth is a muscle full of other muscles.

All I ask for is a door that won't lock, but
we take what we can get. I make a frame,
a window, with both pointers and thumbs.

Inside, the world as I want it to be: red cedar
wearing the sun like a halo, licorice ferns unrolling.

The wind combing knots out of my hair. I try to think
perfectible thoughts, but can't choose between the toil

and the trouble. Is something always better than nothing?
Don't answer that. The fog thinks itself into lifting.

THE PHOTO SHOOT

I am told to sidle up
to a tree; I ask its limbs

to surround my own
with leaves. There is a clothing there

is a clothing. Under a canopy of lenses
I subvert myself. I am almost

invisible. If my eyes dilated,
they would be two acorns.

There is something
about the veins and pores of flora

that my body responds to
by becoming unseen, becoming

too small to see; what's left
are a few bobby pins

and one clavicle. It might be
another body's branch.

The thing that's difficult
is the timing of it all. Knowing

when to breathe. Knowing when
to do anything, to ask for water,

for a robe or a mirror, to ask for a mirror.
To ask for proof of the shot,

of the shoot that emerged
years after my body left.

FIELD REPORT

The fig fits snugly in your fist. Today's lesson: if it bleeds milk, it's not ripe.

A secret boasts of itself. I don't take the bait. Instead, I'm generous with my embraces; every sleeve in the world is mine to touch. My glass is perpetually half-full until, of course, it's not.

Tonight I struggle to name the constellations. Online, a note that reads, *Please add me to your network.*

Is it possible to ask for something else? If so, what?

I brush my hair with my fingers. I wish I knew the body's secrets. Feeling so helpless, hands in shallow pockets, clenched, then un-.

RAT RACE

I'm trying to keep up, but I'm not trying hard enough.
I move out of the left lane to let others cruise by
on the darkening road to anywhere else.

Elsewhere's always a seductive idea—an idea
that isn't fooling anyone. This place is full of exhaust,

big rigs barreling down every lane. O Fortuna!
Take me away from the traffic of it all: to Three Egg,

Florida, then Andalusia, then to the Isle of Skye.
I'm afraid it's too late to say hello to the new.
"You're not fooling anyone!" I shout to the moon.

From up there, these cars look exactly the same. Trails
of headlights for miles, jewels in a blacked-out landscape.

From the sky, every nest egg looks pretty much the same.
The screech owl eats whatever her talons can snag—

darting mice, a vole or two—but she can't be blamed
for those little deaths. Survival, and its costs, is hard enough
to keep up with. I move the mirror back to where I like it.

EASY DOES IT

The dentist is tired of mouths; the mower,
tired of grass. In the same way, I turn page
after page, looking for some new thrill.

The habit is consoling; each sheet of this book
is secured to the spine. In the reclining chair,
the expert says I won't lose the tooth.

Of course, there are exceptions to every rule.
Things split into most and least desirable:
the weeds or the wacker, Novocaine or the drill.

Despite all precautions, the needle nicks
a nerve. Numbness a kind of monotony.
Will I feel anything ever again? Answer: maybe not.

I said it before, and I'll say it forever:
the tree has bark for a reason. Nothing ever
does it easy. Blink twice if you're fine.

It's hard to cry out with a mouth full of hands.
Do no harm, the bulldozer yells,
then razes your home to the ground.

BROOD PARASITE

I cannot be trusted to live and learn.
I lay my egg, the size of a thumbnail, in my rival's nest.

I lay my egg, thumbnail-sized, in my rival's nest.
Even in the woods, you have to choose a side.

Especially in the woods, you have to choose a side.
Which egg is yours? Your guess is as good as mine.

Whose eggs these are we can only guess. The sparrow
feeds the cowbird; a warbler raises the common cuckoo.

The warbler feeds a cuckoo. You can't always get what you want.
I am the *Who* in *Whodunit*, the cuckoo mother on her own,

preening her feathers, a whodunit on her own. But
look inside the cougar's mouth: beauty's only sometimes free.

Just look inside her mouth. Beauty's almost never free.
I can't trust either of us to learn or to live with it.

THE MIRAGE IS A HOTEL FOR SEEING

Outside the city, rattle weed snags the trash. Night and its millions
of pamphlets, every kind of advertisement. It is Saturday,

and Vegas is a hot wire strung above a chlorine pool,
a bulb surrounded by nothing. There are women nearby. They glitter

for you; they sing as if undoing their husbands' belt buckles.
Ambivalence is a mumbling groom, fixing his gaze on the bridesmaids;

none of these women are fathomable. Leave the open bar, the pool
tables, the girls willing to do everything. Leave the salt, the air dividing;

the taxi with its ignition humming, this penthouse shiny and blank
as Nevada, and the earth surrounding, willing silence.

THE FOG

If we ask how the enlightenment ends,
we're told to ask a different question.

Language isn't our first language.
These tongues are speaking in tongues.

Any hour, any day: the buzzard doesn't flinch
at the oncoming car. Soon as we've passed,
he's back to picking at the dead.

Has the great experiment failed?
Is the dream as we've known it now over?
Behind the curtain's another curtain.

To strike a tone of hope, or loss, or loss
of hope—I've got too many cards in my hand.

Soon these chords start to sound the same,
though when played on different instruments,
they all sound equally wacko.

Not everything's a metaphor.
The thickest fog isn't even visible.

To make it through the cloudiest day,
I conceal my weapon on the roof of my mouth.
The split tongue of a snake—you know,

I don't have to tell you this—
can do more than simply hiss.

AFTER THE FACT

After the fact comes the fiction. The cloak of false clothing,
wolf-man in wool, stalking his prey on the path through the woods.

After the fact comes the belief in anything but. Comes the fib,
the sham, the spectacular trick. A sure ruse, those false lashes

glued to each lid, batting to draw everyone's look. After the loss
of the real comes the close call with feeling—then the fake-out,

the one-two, the roar of the crowd at truth, face-first in the dirt.
But even the fire-eater knows there's no profit in eating fire.

You who pulled the wool: we know where you came from. After
the fiction, the fact comes back. The fire will take care of the fire.

DOMESTIC NOIR

My hands are simple as mice
and harnessed to a body of straw.
The cup you fell into
fell into silence.

To the thimble, the thumb is enormous;
to the thumb, the thimble is snug.
We're uneasy
in the spaces we inhabit.

Hey, cupboard: I dare you to keep
all those secrets.
From the gutter of your wooden sea
fly the moths that run their mouths

all over town—wing-beat,
dust light, too too close.
Shut the door to this room,
empty as a sling enfolding no bone.

GRAMOPHONE

Inside the night and its closets,
you keep company with a handful of noise.

The thin universe gets up and goes.

From argument, evening;
from evening, night,

then the long walk toward the self.

Listen—I try not to stay put.
But let's face it: you always hang out

under a cloud of your own making,

and it's my rooms
you've wandered through,

forever leaving the scene of someone else's crime.

Well, guess what? Heart's a heated thing,
a scar un-repaired, not prepared for the knife.

Hello, storm, I'm your friend, too;

the sky not waving back, a deliberate machine
leaving my life the way it is—

scratch that. The way it was meant to be:

each letter read to the tune
of its own applause,

every darkness ignoring a knob.

DOOR

And what if the mind doesn't have an eye?

If instead the mind has a mouth,
teeth gnawing unchewable cud,

forever mulling the perpetual X.

What's spat is a thought. It lands in the grass.

Then the mind moves on. A finger taps a table;
somebody opens a door.

If the eye that wants to see is blind,
the brain's not a cinema, it's a taste test—

hint of wood and almonds,
dill, pepper, smoke;

your father not a visage but a voice
low and hollow, a bellows on the fire,

then a lock of hair in a fist felt by nails—

not the shape of a shoe horn,
but the scent of unbearable cedar

slamming the door shut.

SKELETON CLOCK

This piece is designed to make its movements visible.
What we don't know about structure will be made explicit.

You see just what I mean: metal is minimal, thinned

and trimmed away to reveal the work beneath the face.
Each escapement, each controlled release of power

is available to the eye. Both winding and unwinding

is vital; only the heart can skip a beat, and the beat
that's skipped will echo on your wrist. If you ask me,

I will tell you: to reassemble the subterranean wheel,

all your fractures must be made known. Here is the bone,
here is the hairspring that causes the wheel to turn,

which controls the gears, the speed of the gears,

and the rate of the movement of hands. Disclosure
is the clock opened up, a vein precisely picking its own lock.

THIEF

In a dream, all the diamonds gone.
You spend years searching
for what's fallen through the floorboards.

Anomaly: everything in its place.
A chair, a book. The window, half-open.

We ask the criminal to explain herself.
Who kept you safe? Where are they now?
A car pulls into the driveway; its engine growls.

You know the answers. The morning's sharp.
Some things are hidden. No one is pure.

DAYLIGHT SAVING

We remove the light from the morning
and place the darkness nearer the night.
We make better use of our time.

There's little room for error.
Is this some kind of joke?
The record's skipping. The needle's stuck.
I know no neighbor's name.

Across the street, a woman drags a can to the curb.
The only pleasure of a list
the crossing off.

I am told not to worry
about that which I cannot change.
Light through a lace curtain speckling the floor.
Yes, you need a steady hand to guide you.

I'm trying to keep up.
This isn't as easy as it looks.
The clock turns back on its own.

FIELD REPORT

On Rattlesnake Hill, the new view is the old view, revised to include a little white noise. Farm machinery, buzz-saw, good work.

Antique store, antique store, gas station, antique store. A road winds around itself; these maps can't keep up. The corner of my eye is full of hills.

Back home, a glass of wine, and then another glass. What people call "the tears of the wine" is basically true.

A stranger calls and says, "Boy, are you hard to get ahold of." For some reason I say, "Peekaboo!" and then hang up.

From the driveway, the snake shakes a dry warning, then slithers back under the house.

JANUARY, HUDDLED

The light is empty of stitching,
of bright weather, bees not opening
from a hole in a tree.

This tongue has a mouth's worth of teeth,
and each one hangs with ice.

In winter
I am the cat with three eyelids,
each one unscrolled to veil
a different feeling.

What I mean is,
the gallery exhibits its own empty walls.

What used to be a voice blew under the door;
outside, one degree of temperature

is a lonely thing to feel.
It's a small world, after all.

MASQUERADE

A tree on its side, painted white,
lying quietly
inside the ice storm.

You shake the snow globe twice for luck.
Things happen and happen again.

Outside, a moth revolves around its own light.

You can't be too careful, I said,
side-eyed—

woeful neighbor,
you know the song.

Where there wasn't rust, you guessed it:

a thumbprint red on glass.

Plant the seed. Sad the dead.
You said it didn't have to be mask time,

but here we are:

me with my fox face,
you with yours. A study in two furs.

With our ritual we raise the dead,

we pull trees up by their roots.
Little shaman, good luck:

your harlequin, your moth,
your fingerprint will sing

when you can't sing anymore.

COLORATURA

Up and down the clouded hallway,
toe to heel to toe,
you're a nettle in a jar and you're ravenous.

Smoke leaves a trail of exhaust, and oak leaves
jewel the trail to your room.

Calling *Ice Queen, Ice Queen,*
the whisperers threaten your body
for nights of waiting.

Meanwhile,
your interior drama continues to play out:

a stricture for a necklace,
a bulb for a voice. And the afternoons

are kidney-colored, are sharp with biting,
with blood-letting leading

to all the wrong epiphanies.
Take the honey, leave the tea,
wave the wasps away.

Refusing the soft grip
of the evening, unzip yourself from your costume

and emerge as a deer, sable-colored,
unbound and bounding away.

BEWILDERMENT

I like how the candle just quits
when the wax and the wick are through.
How the smoke slips up the chimney;
how the laundry loves a wind.

I am an absent driver, scanning the sky for a hawk
and the woods for a deer. None to be seen.
Instead the larch, flaming against the dark;
sunbeam through a keyhole, sharp on the floor.

How long did you say we've lived here?
You thought you heard your voice;
I know I heard my name.
Something disturbs the dresses on the line.

Friends, the ghosts persist. Between us
and the world they build a soft promenade,
where hide and seek becomes *Save yourself.*
Where bewilderment is the easiest dilemma.

DOMESTIC NOIR

Light cuts through the kitchen
and lands on a knife;
a braid of bread unravels.
Your eyes simmer.
A thousand Julys are over,
leaving us limping into August,
our fists full of matches.
I want to bite the hand that feeds me.

What were you *thinking?* someone asks—
close the piano
so it's never played again.
Listen instead to the breeze
doing battle with the curtains,
to the bell banging loudly
in your head. Swing hard at the air,
pummel the pillow.
This house is no place
for unsung singing.

SUMMER, LATER

In the earliest version of this morning's ballad

I built a yellow room. I'm listening to the sun from the outside in,
placing a stethoscope to its skin. It's August;

I don't want to own a single voice. It's true, my eyes

have built up a resistance to sunrise.
Something besides a door is ajar—

there's a wind, and a wind, then a crow. Now
both our throats swing open, bell to bell.

Day, how long will you last? I wish the life

back into the yellowing paint. It's never the stars
we find in the sky. Instead it's the red-eyed bird,

a flame recreating its own flowers.

THAT OUR DESIRE IS INCREASED BY DIFFICULTY

Beethoven lays his head on the piano. The listener looks away.

A circle of sportsmen closes in on the doe.

The sky is hostile, the sky is hostile, the forest
one of many sounds that won't move.

Stuck in the arm of the unclouded day, I whyed and I whyed;
I asked the moon to eat the sun

and the river, for once, to stand still.

Under a cloak of fake night, the thief bypasses what's open
and goes straight for the locked door.

While Vronsky pours a drink, Anna watches the oncoming train.

Unclose your eyes, wanderer: that's a way, too,
of refusing relief,

a way of sharpening the knife
while you thunder out a song.

Body of wood, be my voice.
If your breath begins to see mine, the fall is coming.

SPEAK OF THE MEADOW

Speak of the meadow and it appears.
Speak of the fox and it's gone.
If, as the philosopher says,
the limits of my language are the limits
of my world, then the world is part comfort,
part threat. The pasture shields, briefly,
the trickster from the hunter.
At the edge of the wood
a flash of red. I can't say what I see.

Speak of the unwanted world
and it speaks back. The sky boils,
but cradles a white sun setting, a firefly
in the jaw of a lynx.
Its tongue curls out, whipping a word
at a child that can't snap back, and
I hear the trees roaring, receding,
blindfolded branches lashing their leaves,
the names themselves nameless.

WISTERIA

Night, you've textured me with sadness.
I don't know what to do
with this unfamiliar shade,
this head full of sagging flowers.

The garden's darkness is a garland
woven with moving.

It's not in your nature
to be sinister, sister,
but you'd strangle the world if it felt right.
You'd substitute the venom for the cure.

Some bouquets frighten me.
In their heads, I imagine, fangs wait.

How to distinguish hysteria
from wisteria, aftermath from ruin?
There's no way to separate
this evening from its dusk.

I will not play the fool.
I will not coax the wax from the bee.

Take me to the morning
that outlasts all other mornings,
that opens on acres of yellow
with no thick petals to speak of;

take me to the dawn that drives the sun
to drag its mirror across the lake
where seeing will no longer be new.

THE CALM EYE PASSES OVER

What begins in a landscape, what begins with the land

A field of hayseed, here is a field

Here is a horse, her neck bent down

A neck that scatters the birds away

There's a form of incomplete mourning

A storm with an eyewall, but no eye

At the blindest hour of night

a woman drags a box to the forest

hurling plate after plate

against the young trees

What a loss comes to mean

Shattered plates in the woods

One after one, the night-blind trees

A very young widow, the porcelain smashed

A shattered plate in the woods

"A very human raindrop"

A human sorrow, some human rain

"I love you, but I can't give you anything"

Like something that doesn't exist

A plate, then its shards in the woods

A plate, then the underside of a word

Try to convince me

the hammer loves the egg

Try to convince me

the eye of the storm is open

That the eye of the storm that sees you

will bypass the cowering form

Where my grief meets your grief

A clear eye

A filled eye

A ragged eye

Grief against the

mourning for the

sorrow at the

hammer

The eyewall meets the forest

A mile-wide eye, a pinhole eye

While the calm eye passes

my grief meets your grief

Eye in an eye, unstable eye

The calm eye passes over

Where the field meets the forest, a very human word

Where my grief meets your grief

the calm eye passes over

AERIAL

January, brightly. You strip the scene of its objects—

windowsill, salt shaker, handkerchief.

Where do I go from here? the cast-off child asks,

and you are that discarded daughter.

Heart-beat, heart-beat, husk.

If you commit something to memory, it will be imperfect—

me and all the rest of me,

orange-haired girls waving goodbye to their childhoods,

we curl up between the ridges of a shell.

In the ear of the whelk, every sound sounds far away.

You took the staircase leading into the sea.

Then you returned, but part of your self was missing.

Like the young thing

who chopped off her own braid,

the question is, *What will you refuse to part with?*

In the next ocean, you'll be many brilliant spells

flung from the end of a wizard's wand,

the sea foam transfigured into thinning air.

LITTLE EPIC

Broom-sky,
wind swept by wind. Clouds
layered simply, as laundry is layered. Making it difficult
to forecast anything.

You gave me
handfuls of the tide's hair.
I took a little epic in the shape of a rowboat,
the shape of a shut eye.

What I want
to remember is the island,
its iron lung, castoff junk. How it was good to me,
not a residue. But what adheres

are fireflies'
scattered lighthouses,
that green blinking. What adheres is your unavailable
beauty. To be without history:

what sea
and what sad wrench,
cranking the waves back against the waves
against the waves.

SEA THISTLE

Sure, you can dream in a room,
but in a coastal pasture, the thistle
does its dreaming for you.

A lovely amnesia, this lack
of what happened yesterday,
or the day before the day before,

all of our belongingness
sewn inside the sleeve
of her silver dress.

Thistle, but no shore in sight.
Spiky symmetry, blue sizzle posing
as every petal.

That's the place I want to be,
alabaster sea
with no shore to worry over—

disorientation
the least of concerns, each hour
a raindrop in reverse—

then the sky, empty and clear.
At the edge of the world,
beauty must be secondary.

AFTER WE FELLED THE NOBLE FIR

After we felled the Noble fir, you washed the sap from my hands. In the sink, the soap and the sap, and a nest, a bed of needles. You read my future in their pattern: *You'll do this, you'll do that. It will be this way.* True, all of this happened: a pair of hands in the mirror, a gathering of dark matter. We traced the lines of pine in the white basin and left the tree outside, a cut thing.

We axed the tree and left it overnight. In the morning, its branches were traced with the evening's weather, each needle made clear by the frost that encased it. In this way I can approach any past: shake the snow from the limbs, bring the body inside.

Somewhere further north, elk wander into the next season and pine needles bend to wind, collecting along the banks of the river. A different kind of departure: a man who locks eyes with a woman in a mirror and will not look away, or the movement through town of a hearse with no body inside.

WHAT REMAINS

There are holes in these rooms, openings
and closings. Cracked doors; air.

Nothing safe from the stain of passage.
For instance, the bathtub draining

water, leaving silt. Drip of soap
on tile, the filmy remainder,

filthy reminder of what is clean
and what remains to be cleaned:

the body and the place left behind
the body, space of wash and dirt.

The houseplant retreats into soil,
small rose of a mouth withdrawing,
dry from want of water.

What remains are the afterthoughts
of need, a few holes among the weeds.

The beauty of another body's wreck
is tied to the bed of belief

in the tides, the coming and going
of what is fluid.

A lack of something loose
speaks, and in speaking, says

how much of wanting
is made of what you are.

GHOST'S GHOST

Say it out loud:

in the machine of bones there's a ghost,
a continually cooling breath

headed elsewhere.
A mouse

builds a burrow
with the bones of a crow,

and in her building
makes a case for rearrangement;

after it expires, repurpose the form.
In every honeycombed structure,

find the ghost's ghost.
Say it out loud;

unsettle the argument,
unmake the bed—

drive past the house
full of history that never happened

then build it, room by room,
door and jamb, bones

and all from memory.

SUNDOWN, SKY

Sundown, sky repeating blackbirds. The leaves of the smoke tree
are plum-dark, each branch a stiletto of exhaust. This land is charged

with my kind of weather, electricity as wide as August, as far as Oklahoma.
Wasps quarrel above thatches of scotch broom, and I am caught staring

at the sun: the locked eye dreams of ruin, of blaze. I am dreaming
of a cabinet of black-eyed Susans blooming in a burned-out house.

Then, out of nothing, an ear; and in the garden, a bird dismembered, wings
subtracted from the body that bore them, its feathers an ash-heap,

disappearing—the plume of the plume, the sun avalanching, even
the scotch broom scorched—whoever said beauty was an undamaged thing?

POEM WITH CLOUD AND TANGERINE

What falls immediately falls without ceremony.

Orange, a navigable lake spilling over
its shores. Meantime: gray and white levitate.

There was a door that opened to my heart

and when it opened, a small ocean stayed put.
Your mouth, too, refused movement,

but your eyes make words. Rehearse, deliberately,

the story of your past. There's a curtain and a cur.
Place a finger to the lips of the dead, then listen.

Keyholes sing cloud-songs. Your life is one of them.

FANTASY IS A PLACE WHERE IT RAINS

Fog settled in to the twenty-first century. We had to live our lives; with our hands we went looking. Leaving the world alone in its noise, we followed the blue fox.

It's one thing to throw caution to the wind, another to entrust oneself to shadows. You were told, many times, to carry breadcrumbs. Storm to traveler: *Don't make me build a weapon out of a water drop.*

Objectivity's impossible. Seeing is feeling, not the other way around. If you find a key to the forest, will you try the lock? Will you fill my piano with water, as I dreamed you would?

USE CABBAGE TO HEAL THE BRUISE

Use cabbage to heal the bruise; use the bruise
to remember damage and the place of damage.
Use a cherry as a way of hiding the stone,
the stone as a method to measure the river.

The river can be used. How you use it is up to you.
Use the cat's purr to patch the ear that hears heartbeat,
the field to rid yourself of sound. The minute is a mode
of recovery. Use its length to count your breath,

then use your breath to remember the window.
A window's memory is weak. Use the sparrow's beak
to peck into a house's past. At night, use shards of glass
to remember the wine, the wine to ignore the breaking.

Use the mind to read the mind, the skin to locate the bone.
Use a bee as a way to retrace the honey, honey
as a way to discover the bee. Use the iris as an eye,
the lash as a door to close against, the dandelion

to map grass and its movements. Use the wind as a wing,
then the staircase to get down to the sea. Use the sea
to forget the staircase, forget the eye, to forget the sparrow
and bruise and the bee. Use the sea to forget the sea.

LAUREL

Women are leaving their men. In other words,
they are writing the story they were afraid to write.

Some fables take years to devise;
others, days. As for me, I take the long way.
I tiptoe through the tulips.

Once transformed into a tree,
the girl can't escape the woods.
Some fresh threat around the bend.

It's not like this with everything.
Most days, I'm at ease in a crowd.
A bowl of fruit becomes, again, a bowl.

You can always flee a forest fire. A tree cannot.
Survival depends upon the nature of the flame.

I know what you're thinking:
everyone's the hero in their own story.

It's true. The laurel's bark is charred
and bristling. Left alone
the tree becomes, again, a tree.

ONCE YOU LEAVE THE FOREST

Once you leave the forest, it forgets you.
I wish I had good news.

From the outside looking in:
trees spread their gossip, green heads
nodding in unison. Keep walking.

Have hope, but no expectations, my mother says. Nonetheless,
I always pull the wrong end of the wishbone.

I place my heart in the hornet's nest.
I rest my head on a cloud.
More often than not, solitude's the answer.

The river can become an answer, too—
the way it invites the wader,
how dipping a toe

becomes standing ankle-deep,
eye level with shore grass, listening for wind
in the darkening sky.

Instead, the trill of a warbler. Like her,
I'm more easily heard than seen. Like a voice

through the water, the things we had forgotten about
return. I wish I may, I wish
I might. The river talks to me all night.

IF NIGHT IS A HOUSE

If night is a house, and I am a child,
I return to my mother every evening.
In our kitchen she jars every fruit

and pickles anything that might be sweet;
she jams the berries, makes jelly of plums,
then stores them on shelves in our basement.

My head curled in sleep, I am an apple's
long spiral of peel and a cupful of sugar.
When day breaks, I slip out; an oyster,
I shuck myself of shell. In other kitchens

I braid the bread; I boil the tears
from every onion. Those uncoiled scrolls
bring out the frailest person in me: all
my thin voices unwrapped, the simple

clothing shed. But if night is a house
and I am a child, I return to my mother
every evening. Tonight she is stewing

tomatoes and humming me back into sleep.
Stored deep in the basement, I am one
curl on her forehead, a sweet pickled thing.

RECIPE FOR RAIN

In dreams you hold the boot that kicked you
under a jar for twenty years;

for twenty years that leather toe holds still.

And like the closet that loves a dress—
a dress that comes and goes—

you lean against the ebb of your own rooms:

one brother forever walking out of the kitchen,
another sailing over the Dakotas

toward a different winter.

I know that in dreams, your floors
are fastened with safety pins,

and your time is spent freeing the spring from its clasp.

But your sister's advice still holds:
reverse the river,

play dead with the dead.

Create a recipe for rain,
then let the clouds break open.

DIORAMA

Remember the sky as a coat you once wore—
a little night music, air through a chandelier.

Remember the wind as a fifth kind of fog,

and the cotton balls hung with twine,
and handmade lanterns suspended above

our little boat, abalone shell with a pearl

for a heart, sailing through a cellophane sea.
The moon, a paperweight stilling

no paper, cradles instead a dandelion seed

in space—practically invisible, like a chess set
on the head of a pin. At times I like to be

a nobody talking about nothing to no one,

to no one. I love the deep echo. So, too, the ocean,
restless at night, shouldered in seaweed,

is the consequence of its own tide.

SHE SEEMED TO ARRIVE SLOWLY

For hours I pulled toward you, sea star—

I was a traveling pause, I went
deliberately across that dark floor.

The sand created clouds of my lungs.
Taking pleasure in holding zero,

my hands stirred the water and made
ornaments of oyster shells.

To charm your five fingers,
I unrolled a song from my ear—

a long signature to know me by,
a dim and dissolving sugar. Star,

you're the evening that's easy to keep near.

HOUSE OF RAIN

I made my house a house of rain;
at night, a house of snow.

I filled the bedrooms with waves.
I emptied the kitchen of fog.

Here, in the aftermath of pleasure,
we follow the sky-pointing rituals
of the black-necked swans.

They slender toward an unknown god,
burrowed inside a star's star. Arrowed
to the sky, their beaks do not waver.

There's something to be said for silence,
for saying as little as possible.

If I have sent a signal of smoke,
if I have read the lichen on the rocks,
tell me: how do we read this new map?

The path indistinguishable from the bramble,
the bramble obscuring the bog.

Let the world have what it wants;
the rain refrains from falling.

New map, same compass.
This earth will outlast us.

FIELD REPORT

For the most part, wind takes its time. The smoke tree notices. Rehearsing for an imaginary recital, cowbirds go back and forth.

Likewise, I've come to rely on every morning's ritual: pull the blinds, start the coffee. Rinse the pot and water the plants. In these habits I share a life with everybody else.

Yesterday, I thrust my key in the door. Guess what? It was open the whole time.

Confession: I am never nearer to knowing what I want. A map of the West one moment, a blanket the next. The smoke tree notices. Its leaves leave room for my desire. The world, we know, is wide open.

FOG FOREST

The blue spruce is a seamstress
of dark dresses. Its needles blink.
You feel small
in your new weather.

To the north, the broad hemlock;
to the south, red cedar sleeping.
You wonder where the other wanderers are,
pockets full of stones, shoes full of leaves.

What does the wind do?
Blows the coat of snow from the sparrow.
And the rain?
Makes a soft monument of moss.

Before you grow old in this poem,
tiptoe through the time you touched
fingertip to fern—leave a crumb,
then drop another. Build a trail

leading back to yourself. Let deer do the work
of wandering; look for the blue
through the hole in the pine. The needle
at the heart of the tree points skyward.

I HOPE THE OWL REMEMBERS ME

In a land of needles and mosses, I want to know what the prey
and the preying bird knows. I will sleep with both eyes open.

Who wants you, little star?
Who wants you, hatchling?

No wind moves the blue evergreen. I cannot find the source of noise.

I know she lives with the moon in her eye,
the hazelnut moon, hazelnut sky, and she sees
the thimbleberry light in mine.

If, like the owl, I could look backward.
If, like the owl, I could mimic the texture of the forest.

Instead I guessed the cryptic plumage,
the beak hooked at the tip for gripping—
but what I want to grasp is the grimmer meaning

of the owl's locking foot, her practically silent flight
and asymmetrical ear.

The bird, of course, is a kind of misdirection—

another way of saying that I will fill my own coffin with bark.
It will be like a nest that knows something.

Treehouse, take back your architecture.
I want to live in the structure of a feather and the gaze
of an absolute eye. When I leave the world

with a sleeping tongue, the door
of the forest slightly open,

I hope the owl remembers me—

the owl I hope
she remembers

CRADLE

The ornaments of winter are taken down
one by one. My mother cutting back the pear tree;
late afternoon, tinsel on the fence.

At last, what feels like home.

We play make-believe in a measuring cup
while the chestnuts rest in a bowl.

Close your eyes and count to ten.
Brush your hair a hundred times.
I say yes. I have no questions.

I'm almost ashamed at the things I love:

rabbits settling into grass,
the grass a willing cradle

and your hands, every now and then,
folding into the shape of a bird.

ROW

When all the boats were leaving
you were still on shore,
waving to your imagined self on board.

After the fanfare is over,
we learn to favor silence.

In 1911, visitors gathered
to view the empty wall
where the Mona Lisa,
stolen, used to hang.

Wild apple, leaves long gone,
how do you nurse
your discomfort?

When the artist closes a door
she paints a door-sized window;

the girl, a slipper in each hand,
rowing toward morning
in her yellow boat.

NOTES

"Brood Parasite" is after Jericho Brown.

The title "That Our Desire Is Increased by Difficulty" is taken from Michel de Montaigne's essay of the same name, and the lines "Under a cloak of fake night, the thief bypasses what's open / and goes straight for the locked door" are a reworking of the following passage from Seneca, from the same essay: "Locked places invite the thief. The burglar passes by what is open."

The title "Fantasy Is a Place Where It Rains" is taken from Italo Calvino's *Six Memos for the Next Millennium*.

The title "I Hope the Owl Remembers Me" is taken from *The Collected Letters of Emily Dickinson*, and the first two lines of "House of Rain" are a reworking of a line in a letter from the same source ("My House is a House of Snow—").

ACKNOWLEDGMENTS

Many thanks to the editors of the following journals, where these poems, at times in different versions or under different titles, first appeared:

8 Poems: "Laurel"
The Adirondack Review: "Cradle"
Bennington Review: "Speak of the Meadow"
Birdfeast: "That Our Desire Is Increased by Difficulty"
Boned: "Ghost's Ghost"
Booth: "After We Felled the Noble Fir"
The Cincinnati Review: "Skeleton Clock"
concīs: "January, Huddled"
Crazyhorse: "I Have No Way with Words," "I Hope the Owl Remembers Me"
decomP: "The Mirage Is a Hotel for Seeing"
Elke: "Coloratura," "Summer, Later"
Fou: "Use Cabbage to Heal the Bruise"
Foundry: "Poem with Cloud and Tangerine"
Grist: "Sundown, Sky" (as "[Sun-down, sky repeating blackbirds]")
The Harpoon Review: "The Calm Eye Passes Over"
Inter|rupture: "Bewilderment"
Jet Fuel Review: "The Photo Shoot," "She Seemed to Arrive Slowly"
Matter: "What Remains" (as "In Exchange, What Remains")
Natural Bridge: "If Night Is a House"
Oxidant Engine: "House of Rain"
Permafrost Magazine: "Field Report" ["The fig fits snugly"], "Field Report" ["On Rattlesnake Hill"]
Radar Poetry: "After the Fact," "Easy Does It," "The Fog," "Once You Leave the Forest," "Wisteria"
Redivider: "Row"
Slippery Elm: "Aerial"
Smartish Pace: "Fog Forest"
Southampton Review: "Little Epic" (as "The Amnesiac and the Anemone")
Sugar House Review: "Gramophone"
Third Coast: "Masquerade"
Thrush: "Door"
Tupelo Quarterly: "Domestic Noir" ["My hands are simple as mice"]
Two Peach: "Recipe for Rain"

I am grateful for support from the Jentel Artist Residency Program, the Ora Lerman Charitable Trust, Artsmith, and the Sundress Academy for the Arts, as many of these poems were written while in residence with these organizations. Thank you for the time and space you give to writers and artists of all stripes.

Many thanks to Lisa Fay Coutley, for her valuable and perceptive reading of an earlier version of this manuscript, and to Mark Irwin and Martha Silano, with much gratitude for their attention and generosity. To Mary Biddinger, Amy Freels, Jon Miller, and the University of Akron Press team for bringing this book to life. To my English and Humanities students and colleagues at Ohio Northern University, many thanks for a wonderful environment in which to work and learn every day.

Much love to friends who have offered encouragement, cheer, and care along the way: Patrick Thomas, Sarah Green, Brian Dickson, Jennifer Pullen, and Rebecca Morgan Frank. To Virginia Konchan, whose fierce editorial support I cherish, whose poems have meant so much to me, and whose friendship I hold dear. To my family far and wide, especially Mom and Dad, and to Diz, and Scrap, and Jeff, my best and forever loves.

Jennifer Moore was born and raised in Seattle. She is the author of *The Veronica Maneuver* (University of Akron Press, 2015) and the chapbook *Smaller Ghosts* (Seven Kitchens Press, 2020). Her poems have appeared in *Crazyhorse, Bennington Review, Interim, The Cincinnati Review,* and elsewhere, and her work has been recognized by residencies with and fellowships from the Jentel Arts Foundation, Artsmith, and the Ora Lerman Charitable Trust. An associate professor of creative writing at Ohio Northern University, she lives in Bowling Green, Ohio.

Printed in the United States
By Bookmasters